Original title:

Sunrise Serenade

Author: Paula Raudsepp

ISBN HARDBACK: 978-1-80560-159-3

ISBN PAPERBACK: 978-1-80560-624-6

A Symphony of Daybreak

Soft whispers of dawn arise,
Birdsongs fill the waking skies.
Gentle light begins to creep,
As the world stirs from its sleep.

Morning dew on blades of grass,
Glistening as the moments pass.
Colors brush the sky so bright,
A canvas painted with pure light.

The horizon blushes warm and fair,
Each heartbeat a silent prayer.
Nature's symphony plays on high,
As daybreak paints the waking sky.

Golden Hues Unfold

Sunrise spills its golden rays,
Illuminating the new day's ways.
Fields awake in amber glow,
Whispers of warmth in breezes flow.

Flowers bloom with colors bold,
In the morning's touch, life unfolds.
Soft petals kissed by light's embrace,
Nature's charm, a timeless grace.

Through the branches, shadows play,
As night gently gives way to day.
Golden hues in the sky so blue,
Each moment a gift, fresh and new.

Radiant Rhapsody

A melody of light appears,
Dancing joy as dawn draws near.
Birds take flight in rhythmic arcs,
Painting stories in the parks.

The sun climbs high, a golden sphere,
Whispers of hope, the heart will hear.
With every beam, the world anew,
Life awakens, fresh with dew.

Echoes of laughter fill the air,
Every moment an answered prayer.
In this rhapsody, hearts entwine,
As nature sings, we feel divine.

Morning's Breath of Hope

With dawn's first light, the shadows fade,
A promise blooms where dreams are laid.
In stillness, every heart can find,
A breath of hope, sweet and kind.

Golden beams touch the earth so gently,
Lighting paths for souls who venture boldly.
A tapestry of colors bright,
Morning whispers soft, igniting light.

In the quiet, a new beginning,
Each heartbeat, a soft song singing.
Hope unfurls with each sunlit ray,
Guiding us through the light of day.

Harmony Among the Clouds

Whispers dance on gentle breeze,
Colors blend with playful ease.
Clouds embrace the softest light,
Painting dreams in pure delight.

High above, where wishes soar,
Silent tales from days of yore.
Together, they float and glide,
In this realm where hopes reside.

Sunset strums a golden tune,
Stars awaken, silver moon.
Harmony in endless skies,
Where the heart forever flies.

Raindrops sing on canvas bright,
Each a note, a spark of light.
Nature's orchestra at play,
Crafting magic every day.

Beneath the arch of sky so wide,
We find solace, peace, and pride.
In the clouds, our spirits roam,
Together, we have found a home.

Radiant Anticipation

Morning breaks with golden rays,
Hope resides in soft embrace.
Birds awaken, sing their song,
Filling hearts, where dreams belong.

Dew-kissed grass, a vibrant hue,
Nature whispers, bright and new.
Every shadow starts to fade,
In this dance of light, we've made.

Time unwinds in gentle flow,
Promises of joy will grow.
With each heartbeat, more we feel,
Radiance that's truly real.

Waves of laughter, warmth combined,
Painting futures intertwined.
Every glance, a spark ignites,
In the air, electric sights.

In this moment, dreams align,
Together, futures intertwine.
Radiant hearts in sweet embrace,
Eager for our sacred space.

The Dawn's Serenade

As night departs, the world awakes,
Softly sung by peaceful lakes.
Echoes whisper through the trees,
Carried forth by morning's breeze.

Golden hues on sleepy hills,
Melodies of nature's thrills.
Every note a gentle sigh,
In the stillness, we can fly.

Time unfolds, a tender sigh,
Underneath the painted sky.
Birds compose a sweet refrain,
Filling hearts with hope, not pain.

Dewdrops glisten, catching light,
Sparkling gems of pure delight.
In the dawn's embrace we find,
Harmony that's intertwined.

As the day begins its sway,
Let our souls be led astray.
In the dawn's serenade, we see,
Whispers of eternity.

Celestial Prelude

Stars awaken in the night,
Constellations shining bright.
Whispers from the vast unknown,
Calling forth our dreams to own.

Galaxies in silent flight,
Painting darkness with their light.
Every twinkle tells a tale,
In the cosmic, we will sail.

Moonlit paths, a journey starts,
Guiding softly, soothing hearts.
In this prelude, we embark,
To discover every spark.

Nebulas in colors blend,
Crafting wishes without end.
Journey forth through worlds unseen,
In this dance, where we have been.

With each heartbeat, we transcend,
In this story with no end.
Celestial dreams we all pursue,
Together, me and you.

Sunlit Whispers

Beneath the golden rays we stand,
A gentle breeze, a soft command.
The leaves do rustle, dance with glee,
As nature hums its melody.

In the garden where flowers bloom,
Colors bright dispel all gloom.
Bees are buzzing, life anew,
In this realm where dreams come true.

The rays of light, they kiss the ground,
Quiet joy in every sound.
As shadows stretch, the day does fade,
Yet magic lingers, never strayed.

Whispers of sunlight in the air,
Remind us always to be fair.
For in this radiant embrace,
We find our hearts, our truest place.

So let us walk this path of gold,
With stories in the light retold.
Together in this sunlit space,
In harmony, we find our grace.

Awakening Nature's Song

The dawn breaks soft, a tender light,
Awakens life from dreams of night.
With every bird that starts to sing,
A symphony of hope takes wing.

The daisies stretch, the dew does glisten,
In every bloom, the earth will listen.
A dragonfly flits through the air,
A fleeting glance, so bright and rare.

The brook flows swift with laughter's sound,
Its bubbling joy knows no bounds.
Each rustling leaf, each buzzing bee,
Tells us tales of wild, free glee.

As sunlight dances on the trees,
Whispers of love blow in the breeze.
The world awakens, spirits high,
In nature's arms, our hearts can fly.

So let us cherish every note,
In this grand song, we too will float.
With every breath, we join the throng,
In the harmony of nature's song.

Breath of the New Day

The sun peeks through the trees,
Gentle whispers in the breeze.
Dewdrops sparkle on the grass,
Time to let the shadows pass.

Birds begin their morning song,
Nature's choir sings along.
Colors dance in radiant hues,
A canvas kissed by morning's dews.

Light spills forth from the east,
A golden feast for all, at least.
Every heart begins to sway,
In the breath of the new day.

Clouds drift in a tender line,
Each moment feels divine.
Awakening, the world feels bright,
Wrapped in soft, embracing light.

Together, we embrace this morn,
A promise in each heart reborn.
With every step, life finds its way,
In the warmth of the new day.

Serenade of the Awakening

Softly breaks the dawn's refrain,
Nature sings, it's not in vain.
Melodies of life arise,
Underneath the painted skies.

Birds in harmony take flight,
Chasing shadows with delight.
Gentle ripples kiss the lake,
In this haven, hearts awake.

The world adorned with shades of gold,
As stories of the night unfold.
Whispers echo, dreams take form,
In this tranquil, waking storm.

Every creature finds its place,
In the rhythm of embrace.
Awakening, the spirit soars,
To the serenades it adores.

Together, under skies so blue,
The symphony of life anew.
With every note, the heart shall sway,
To the serenade of the day.

Chorus of First Light

In the silence, soft and clear,
Whispers come, drawing near.
A chorus sung by morning's grace,
Filling every empty space.

The horizon holds a glow,
As shadows dance, setting slow.
Rustling leaves, a gentle sigh,
As the sun begins to rise.

Voices rise from every nook,
In the warmth, the world unshook.
Each moment lingers, pure delight,
In the chorus of first light.

Golden rays embrace the dew,
Breaking night with colors true.
Hands held high to greet the day,
In the light, we find our way.

The melody of life begins,
In every heart, the song spins.
Together, we shall sing and write,
To the chorus of pure light.

Morning's Canvas Unfurled

Brushstrokes of the dawn unfold,
A masterpiece in hues of gold.
Each ray, a tale of hope and cheer,
On morning's canvas, bright and clear.

Strokes of pink and softest blue,
Awakening the hearts anew.
Every shadow starts to part,
As light begins to play its part.

Dewdrops glisten, nature's art,
A tender echo of the heart.
With every brush, the day awakes,
In the beauty that it makes.

Birds take flight in graceful arcs,
Painting joy with vibrant sparks.
In this moment, feel it all,
Let the morning's magic call.

Together, let us seize the day,
On this canvas, come what may.
With every breath, we shall unfurl,
The beauty of the morning's world.

Celestial Revelations

Beneath the vast and starry sky,
The whispers of the night unfold.
Each twinkling light, a silent sigh,
In mysteries both bright and bold.

A comet trails its shimmering plume,
As dreams take flight on cosmic waves.
In the silence, shadows bloom,
And time itself, the secret saves.

Galaxies dance in ancient waltz,
While planets spin in graceful grace.
Their beauty found in every pulse,
An endless journey through deep space.

Through telescopes, we dare to glance,
At stories written long ago.
In every spark, there lies a chance,
To learn what stars may choose to show.

Celestial hearts in vibrant hue,
Illuminate the darkened night.
We seek the truth the heavens strew,
In every dream, we chase the light.

The Joy of New Beginnings

When morning rays in silver gleam,
And dew-kissed petals greet the dawn,
A whisper stirs, a tender dream,
In every heart, a fresh new song.

With every step, the world awakes,
As hope unfurls in warming light.
The path ahead, a dance it makes,
With promise shining ever bright.

A seedling breaks the soil's embrace,
Reaching upwards toward the sun.
In nature's arms, we find our place,
And feel the joy of life begun.

So let us cast away our fears,
And open wide our boundless wings.
In laughter, joy, and maybe tears,
The genius of our spirits sings.

For every end, a new start waits,
In every turn, a door shall close.
Embrace the thrill that life creates,
And rise once more, as fortune grows.

Harmonies of the First Light

The dawn breaks soft, with gentle hues,
A symphony unheard before.
Each ray of sun, a note infused,
In melodies that we explore.

The world awakes in vibrant tones,
With every bird that takes to flight.
In whispers soft, the earth intones,
The harmony of waking light.

Flowing streams hum their sweet refrain,
While blossoms sway in breezy dance.
Each moment holds a joy unchained,
In nature's grand and tender glance.

Embrace the dawn, let shadows fade,
For light reveals what night conceals.
With every sunlit serenade,
The soul ignites and truly feels.

Together we will sing anew,
In every heartbeat, find our way.
With love and joy, we'll travel through,
And greet each dawn as bright as day.

Melodic Hues of Awakening

Awake, arise, the time is near,
To find the colors yet unseen.
In every shadow, lend an ear,
To whispers soft where dreams have been.

The canvas of the dawn is spread,
In vibrant strokes, a lively sight.
With every brush, new visions tread,
A tapestry of pure delight.

The laughter of the trees resounds,
As sunlight weaves through green and gold.
In every rustle, life abounds,
And tales of old begin retold.

Each step we take, a note that sings,
In symphonies of earth and sky.
With open hearts, we spread our wings,
And bid the sleeping world goodbye.

So let us paint the day anew,
With every hue our spirits crave.
In every moment, dreams come true,
Awake, arise, be truly brave.

Morning's Ecstasy

The sun peeks over hills, so bright,
Whispers of dawn, a gentle sight.
Birds sing sweetly in melody,
Nature awakens, wild and free.

Dewdrops glisten on blades of grass,
Every moment, time seems to pass.
Colors bloom in vibrant hues,
Morning's joy, a cherished muse.

Clouds drift lazily through the blue,
Kissing the earth, a tranquil view.
Breezes carry the scent of spring,
Hope and life in each new thing.

A canvas of dreams painted wide,
In every heart, where peace resides.
Awake, arise to greet the day,
In morning's light, let worries sway.

With open arms, the world unfolds,
Stories shared, adventures told.
Together, let us dance and sway,
In morning's ecstasy, we'll stay.

Tapestry of Dawn

Threads of light weave through the trees,
Softly stirring with the breeze.
Morning stretches, yawning wide,
Colors blend, dreams coincide.

Each ray dances on the lake,
A mirrored glow, the world awake.
Birds take flight in glorious arcs,
Painting sky with joyful sparks.

Whispers of night fade away,
As warmth spills in, bursting day.
Fog retreats in gentle sighs,
Revealing secrets held in skies.

Nature unfolds her lush embrace,
Inviting all to find their place.
Underneath the vast expanse,
Life begins anew, a chance.

Tangled roots and petals fair,
Life's tapestry woven with care.
In every hue, create your song,
For dawn's melody will make you strong.

Symphony of Awakening

The world stirs softly from its sleep,
As sunlight starts its gentle leap.
Each note rings clear, announcing day,
In harmony, we find our way.

A chorus swells among the trees,
Nature's pulse a steady breeze.
Rustling leaves and chirping calls,
In symphony, the morning sprawls.

Golden rays cascade like streams,
Waking weary hearts and dreams.
Misty clouds drift far and wide,
A canvas where hopes are tied.

As shadows fade and colors blend,
Each heartbeat marks a fresh new trend.
Life awakens in vibrant hue,
In this symphony, we renew.

With every step, the world does sing,
Embracing joy that mornings bring.
Together, let us raise our voice,
In a symphony, we rejoice.

Mirth of the Morning

Laughter lingers on the breeze,
Morning smiles, a heart that sees.
With every dawn, a chance to play,
In the mirth of the everyday.

Sunshine spills across the land,
Nature offers a gentle hand.
Colors chirp in sunny tones,
A playful dance among the stones.

Joy spills forth like blooming flowers,
In every moment, feel life's powers.
Awake, arise, let's seize the time,
In this morning's radiant rhyme.

Winds of laughter lift our souls,
In the light, only joy consoles.
With friends and family by our side,
In morning's mirth, we take our ride.

Together, hearts entwined and free,
Reveling in life's tapestry.
Celebrate each dawn's debut,
For in morning's mirth, we grow anew.

Light's Embrace on Earth

Morning rays softly glow,
Kissing the dew-soaked grass.
Nature wakes from slumber,
Whispering secrets that last.

Flowers stretch towards the sun,
Petals dance in gentle breeze.
Life awakens with each ray,
In a world that aims to please.

Birds sing a joyful tune,
Their melodies fill the air.
Each note a celebration,
Of beauty found everywhere.

Trees sway with ancient grace,
Shadows play upon the ground.
In this embrace of warmth,
Every heartbeat is profound.

Sunset drapes the evening,
Casting colors that inspire.
Light's embrace on Earth is pure,
A canvas set on fire.

Day's First Breath

Whispers of dawn arise,
As night bids a soft adieu.
Golden light spills through trees,
Awakening skies of blue.

The world begins to stir,
With the softest sighs of morn.
Each leaf a gentle shiver,
As the day is reborn.

Birds chirp, a sweet chorus,
In harmony with the breeze.
Nature's lullaby unfolds,
Bringing peace and gentle ease.

Clouds drift like cotton candy,
Bright against the azure hue.
With every moment passing,
There's promise in all that's new.

Day's first breath is magic,
A moment we hold dear.
In this fleeting sunrise,
Hope and joy reappear.

Golden Glimmers Above

Stars twinkle in the night,
Whispers of ancient lore.
Each one a tiny beacon,
Guiding dreams forevermore.

Moonlight bathes the landscape,
In a silver soft embrace.
Eyes turned skyward in wonder,
Lost in this celestial space.

Constellations tell stories,
Of heroes, myths, and grace.
In their light, we find solace,
A momentary embrace.

Galaxies swirl in silence,
In a dance across the skies.
Infinite dreams entwined,
Underneath these vast goodbyes.

Golden glimmers above,
Sparkling like hopes reborn.
In the tapestry of night,
We find peace in every dawn.

Awakened Wonders

In the forest deep and wide,
Where sunlight barely shines,
Awakened wonders flourish,
In nature's storied vines.

Creatures stir amidst the leaves,
A rush of life cascades.
Each step a new adventure,
In muted, dappled glades.

Streams murmur their secrets,
As they weave through ancient stone.
Nature's chorus sings softly,
In harmony, never alone.

Mountains cradle the horizon,
Standing tall, steadfast, and free.
Guardians of these wonders,
Whispering eternally.

Awakened wonders beckon,
Inviting hearts to roam.
In their embrace, we find peace,
A place that feels like home.

Revelry of the Break of Day

Dawn whispers secrets to the night,
Stars fade softly, losing their light.
Colors burst in a golden display,
Nature awakens, welcoming the day.

Birds take flight in joyful song,
Chasing shadows that dare not belong.
Morning's breath, crisp and clear,
Promises of new dreams draw near.

The sun creeps up, a fiery sphere,
Painting the world, vanquishing fear.
Joy spills forth from every tree,
As life begins its revelry.

Fields adorned with dew's embrace,
Each droplet holds a fleeting grace.
A symphony of laughter and cheer,
In nature's arms, we hold what's dear.

With each moment, time reclaims,
The magic found in morning's games.
Celebrate the light, let it stay,
In the revelry of the break of day.

Echoes of the New Horizon

Whispers of change dance on the breeze,
Carried forth with grace and ease.
The horizon stretches, wide and free,
Inviting dreams in jubilant spree.

Mountains stand tall, a silent might,
Guardians watching the fading night.
Clouds parade with a painted dream,
Reflecting what the heart may deem.

The sun rises, a fiery embrace,
Illuminating each crevice and space.
Waves of hope lap at the shore,
A chorus of visions, forevermore.

The call of adventure fills the air,
Awakening spirits that long to dare.
With every heartbeat, new paths we chart,
Echoes of courage resound in the heart.

Chasing shadows, unveiling the light,
We stand together, ready for flight.
In the promise of dawn's brand new song,
We find our place where we belong.

Palette of the Rising Sky

Brushstrokes of orange kiss the blue,
A canvas unfolding, fresh and new.
The pastel hues bloom in delight,
Awakening dreams in morning light.

Clouds drift lazily, soft and white,
Carrying whispers of day and night.
Nature's palette, a wondrous blend,
Colors converge, horizons extend.

Birds glide through the painted air,
Chasing the sun, free without care.
Light spills forth, a joyous tide,
A masterpiece where hopes abide.

In this moment, time stands still,
Over hills and valleys, a vibrant thrill.
Every shade tells a story untold,
In the palette of the rising sky bold.

As day unfolds, the colors may change,
Yet the beauty remains, never strange.
Each dawn a gift, wrapped in hues,
A dance of light we forever choose.

Footsteps in the Morning Dew

Softly the world begins to wake,
With every sound, the silence breaks.
Footsteps lead through the glistening grass,
Where echoes of dreams in dew drops pass.

Whispers of fragrance from blooms nearby,
Awakening senses beneath the sky.
Each step a promise, soft and true,
In the tender morn where life renews.

A delicate tapestry, woven tight,
Through nature's wonders, bathed in light.
The earth sighs gently, a loving sigh,
As footprints linger, time drifting by.

In the cool embrace of day's first rays,
We spark our souls in a hopeful blaze.
With gratitude held in every view,
We wander forth in morning's dew.

The journey unfolds with every stride,
In the soft glow where dreams reside.
Our footsteps echo, serene and clear,
In the morning's embrace, we hold what's dear.

Awakening the Earth

Beneath the dawn's soft glow,
Flowers bloom and rivers flow,
Gentle whispers fill the air,
Nature stirs, free from care.

Mountains rise against the sky,
Birds take wing, a joyful cry,
Awakening the slumbering trees,
Dancing lightly in the breeze.

Golden rays of sun do pour,
Touching gently on the floor,
Of a world that breathes anew,
Life's sweet promise breaking through.

In the fields, the grass does sway,
As the night gives way to day,
Every creature, large and small,
Feels the earth's enchanting call.

Harmony in every sound,
Whispers of the sacred ground,
As we greet this vibrant sphere,
Awakening, we revere.

Twilight's Farewell

The sun sinks low, a golden hue,
Whispers of night bid adieu,
Stars emerge in tranquil grace,
As shadows dance, we find our place.

A gentle breeze begins to sigh,
Crickets sing their lullaby,
Moonlight drapes the sleepy land,
Casting dreams like grains of sand.

In twilight's arms, the world does pause,
Reflecting on the day's applause,
Every moment softly glows,
In the calm where quiet flows.

The horizon blushes, faint and bold,
As secrets of the night unfold,
Embracing stars, a silver thread,
In twilight's grasp, no words are said.

Farewell to day, the twilight gleams,
We wander softly into dreams,
With painted skies and whispered night,
Together we embrace twilight's light.

Symphony of Light

In a world where colors blend,
Radiant rays around us send,
Nature's tapestry unfolds,
A symphony of light retold.

Golden sun on waters gleams,
Chasing softly all our dreams,
Every hue, a note in time,
Playing out in perfect rhyme.

Through the trees, the sunlight weaves,
Casting shadows, the heart believes,
A dance of light in endless flight,
Filling souls with pure delight.

Whispers of the dawn arise,
Painting clouds in pastel skies,
As evening falls, the colors blend,
A symphony that has no end.

In every glimmer, hope takes flight,
A heartbeat in the quiet night,
Together we find joy and grace,
In this bright and sacred space.

Embracing the New Day

With the dawn, we greet the morn,
A fresh embrace, the world reborn,
Nature's canvas, bright and clear,
Inviting us to draw near.

Echoes of yesterday fade,
While new adventures are displayed,
Birds awaken with their songs,
In this flow where life belongs.

Each moment's gift, we carry forth,
In the warmth that speaks of worth,
Sunbeams dance upon our skin,
Celebrating where we begin.

Open hearts, we learn to see,
The beauty in what's yet to be,
Together we will strive and play,
Embracing the light of the new day.

In unity we stand as one,
As life unfolds, like morning sun,
With open arms, we find our way,
In the joy of each new day.

Unfolding the Day

A golden hue spills across the sky,
Awakening dreams that softly lie.
Birds sing melodies, pure and sweet,
As daylight dances on waking feet.

The world unfolds, a canvas bright,
Each moment brimming with silent light.
Clouds drift lazily, a painter's brush,
Creating beauty in the morning hush.

Nature whispers secrets in the breeze,
Rustling leaves, swaying trees.
The sun ignites hope's gentle spark,
Leading hearts from the shadows dark.

Time flows slowly, a gentle stream,
Awakening thoughts, igniting dreams.
Each breath, a gift, a chance to be,
In this moment, we are truly free.

Notes of the New Dawn

With every dawn, new notes arise,
A symphony wrapped in golden skies.
Softly played on nature's stage,
The morning's tune, wisdom's page.

Dewdrops sparkle like tiny stars,
Each glimmer whispering from afar.
In the hush, the world sings low,
A melody of hope, gentle and slow.

Colors blend in perfect peace,
As shadows fade, chaos cease.
The horizon paints a tranquil sight,
A promise born of day from night.

Eager hearts open wide,
Embracing warmth that cannot hide.
In every note, a story spun,
As a new day has just begun.

Whispers of the New Horizon

Whispers carried on the gentle breeze,
Secrets of the world among the trees.
The horizon calls with open arms,
Inviting hearts to explore its charms.

Colors merge in a soft embrace,
As the sun rises, setting the pace.
Mountains stand tall, witnesses of time,
Holding stories within their climb.

Each step forward, a promise made,
With every shadow that starts to fade.
Horizons stretch, limitless and wide,
In the light of morning, we take pride.

Dreams take flight on wings of dawn,
Chasing the shadows that linger on.
The world awaits with bated breath,
In the quiet hush, we conquer death.

Embrace of the Morning Mist

Wrapped in mist, the morning sighs,
Soft and tender under painted skies.
The world, a canvas, fresh and new,
Awakens slowly, kissed by dew.

The air is cool, a gentle caress,
Nature blooms, wearing her best dress.
Whispers linger in the silken haze,
As time unfolds in a dreamy daze.

Mountains loom like giants, proud,
Cloaked in mist, beneath a shroud.
Promises echo in the silence found,
In this embrace, love knows no bound.

Hearts awaken with every sigh,
Grateful for the blessings that fill the sky.
Each moment holds a sacred bliss,
In the embrace of the morning mist.

Radiant Promise Unfurled

Beneath the sky, a new day wakes,
With embers bright as morning breaks.
Each ray a whisper, soft and pure,
A tranquil heart, a hope secure.

Flowers bloom in gentle cheer,
As sunlight dances, drawing near.
The world ignites in hues of gold,
A tale of warmth, forever told.

Birds ascend with joyful song,
In the embrace where dreams belong.
Nature sings a vibrant tune,
Her voice a gift, a sacred boon.

Shadows fade as light beams flow,
In every heart, a deeper glow.
Together we'll journey through the light,
Hand in hand, our spirits bright.

So let us stand, our promise true,
With eyes of wonder, grateful view.
In unity, we rise, we twirl,
Embracing life, radiant promise unfurled.

Dawn's Colorful Overture

A canvas spread with shades so bold,
As dawn unfolds its tales untold.
A symphony of light takes flight,
In every gleam, pure delight.

The sky awakens, brushed in pink,
Where thoughts of dreams begin to link.
With every hue, a chance anew,
Horizons gleam with morning dew.

Whispers ride the gentle breeze,
Stirring hopes among the trees.
Nature's chorus, soft and sweet,
Each note a step, life's rhythmic beat.

Clouds embrace the rising sun,
As shadows play and daylight's won.
Each heartbeat echoes grace and peace,
In this dance, we find release.

So let the colors paint our soul,
In perfect harmony, we feel whole.
With open hearts, our spirits soar,
In dawn's embrace forever more.

Serenade for the New Light

As moonlight fades, a chime of gold,
A serenade of love unfolds.
Each note a promise, soft and bright,
Welcoming the tender light.

The stars retreat, their work complete,
With every breath, our hearts entreat.
In the silence, joy awakes,
A melody that never breaks.

Fields of dreams under the sky,
Adorn the night as breezes sigh.
The darkness yields to morning's grace,
In this sweet, enchanting space.

Awakening souls, we rise and share,
In laughter's echo, tender care.
With each heartbeat, time takes flight,
In this serenade for new light.

So let us sing, both near and far,
Together we'll shine, our guiding star.
For in the dawn, we find our tune,
A harmony beneath the moon.

Skyward Symphony

Above the world, a canvas bright,
Painted dreams in shades of light.
Clouds dance in rhythm, pure and free,
A skyward song, our destiny.

With wings of hope, we take to flight,
Chasing visions, hearts alight.
The breeze will carry every sound,
In this embrace, our joy is found.

Oceans watch as mountains sway,
In unity, we seize the day.
The sun will guide our upward quest,
With every heartbeat, we are blessed.

Galaxies swirl in radiant grace,
As we lose ourselves in endless space.
Harmony sings from every star,
Reflecting all that we truly are.

So lift your gaze and feel the air,
With every breath, let dreams declare.
In this symphony, together, we soar,
A skyward dance forevermore.

Ember Hues of Dawn

The sun peeks through the trees,
Painting skies with amber glow.
Whispers of a new day rise,
In the calm where shadows flow.

Birds begin their morning song,
As dew-kissed grass shimmers bright.
Nature wakes with gentle grace,
Embracing the soft morning light.

Clouds melt into shades of fire,
A tapestry of gold and rose.
Time to shed the night's embrace,
With every breath, life's warmth flows.

Waves of color dance and sway,
In the breeze that stirs the air.
Hearts awaken with the dawn,
Freeing dreams without a care.

Embers fade, yet hope remains,
In the light, we find our way.
Every moment, rich and bright,
Guides us gently through the day.

Elysian Morn

A symphony of silver light,
Cascades upon the dew-kissed ground.
Echoes of a world reborn,
Where whispers of the past resound.

Softly blooms the fragrant rose,
In gardens kissed by morning's breath.
In this realm of shimmering peace,
Each moment holds the charm of death.

Morning glory climbs the gate,
With petals speaking tales untold.
Every leaf, a story woven,
In colors bright and vivid gold.

Honeyed sunbeams break the chill,
Embracing all with tender touch.
Hearts open wide, forgetting pain,
In the magic that means so much.

Elysian morn, a sacred space,
Where time stands still, yet flows like streams.
In the arms of this pure dawn,
We awaken to our dreams.

Awakening Dreams

In the twilight of the night,
When stars begin to fade away,
A shimmer stirs within our hearts,
As night gives way to the day.

Thoughts like shadows start to wane,
Lost in whispers of the breeze.
A canvas waiting to be filled,
With dreams that dance among the trees.

Glimmers of hope break through the dark,
As morning light begins to creep.
The world awakens from its slumber,
In secrets that the dawn will keep.

Every heartbeat, strong and true,
Calls forth visions waiting near.
In this moment, all feels right,
Awakening without a fear.

Awakening dreams, once so far,
Now a whisper in our ear.
We embrace the light of dawn,
As possibilities draw near.

Mosaic of Colors Above

The sky, a canvas wide and vast,
Painted with hues both bold and bright.
A mosaic of colors above,
As day gives way to night's soft light.

Brushstrokes of orange and blue,
Blend gently with whispers of gray.
Miracles unfold in the skies,
As sun bids a warm farewell to day.

Stars emerge like distant dreams,
Knitting stories in the night.
Every twinkle, a promise kept,
In the tapestry of starlit flight.

Clouds drift like thoughts on the wind,
Shapes shifting in a soft ballet.
Each moment holds its magic close,
Painting life in a vibrant array.

A mosaic of colors divine,
Captures hearts and lifts the soul.
In the beauty of this horizon,
We find the dreams that make us whole.

Light Breaking Through Shadows

In the quiet dawn of day,
Soft light begins to play.
Shadows dance and twist away,
Bringing warmth where dreams lay.

Golden rays on dewdrops shine,
Banish night, make hearts align.
Whispers of the sun divine,
In their glow, our hopes entwine.

Colors spill from heaven's seam,
Crafting visions like a dream.
Every hue, a gentle beam,
Painting life in every theme.

As the world wakes from its night,
A symphony of pure delight.
With each moment, spirits fight,
Finding solace in the light.

Hope emerges, fresh and bright,
Guiding us with pure insight.
All the darkness takes its flight,
In the dawn's embracing sight.

Melodies of the Aurora

In the night where colors play,
Dancing lights in vast array.
Whispers of the winds convey,
Melodies that softly sway.

Crimson, green, and shades of gold,
A canvas bright, a tale retold.
Nature's tunes, both brave and bold,
In this wonder, hearts unfold.

Beneath the stars, a silent plea,
Listen close, let spirit free.
In each hue, a harmony,
Binding earth and sky in glee.

Songs of light, the universe sings,
Woven tales on cosmic wings.
Every flash, a truth it brings,
In the dark, the heart still clings.

As the dawn begins to break,
Shadows flee, illusions shake.
In the silence, dreams awake,
With the gift that dawn will make.

Radiance Over Hills

Above the hills, the sun ascends,
Painting skies where daylight bends.
Golden light, the silence lends,
To every heart, the magic sends.

Gentle breezes whisper low,
As the world begins to glow.
Blossoms open, rivers flow,
In the warmth, our spirits grow.

Echoing through valleys wide,
Nature's beauty cannot hide.
With each ray, the shadows slide,
In this light, we take our ride.

Mountains catch the glowing flame,
Bearing witness, none the same.
In this dance, we feel no shame,
All are one, and love's the name.

Radiance wraps the earth anew,
In its essence, life shines through.
Hearts united, pure and true,
Under skies of vibrant blue.

The Dawn's Tender Song

As the night begins to fade,
Soft and sweet, a serenade.
Notes of hope in skies arrayed,
In the dawn, our fears are laid.

Gentle light drapes over trees,
Carrying whispers on the breeze.
Every heart finds newfound ease,
In the warmth, the spirit frees.

Birds take flight, their voices rise,
Melodies that touch the skies.
In the stillness, love complies,
With every note, the soul replies.

Colors blend, a soft embrace,
Filling time with gentle grace.
In this moment, we find place,
In the dawn's most tender face.

Let us bask in morning's glow,
Savor every tranquil flow.
In this song, we learn to grow,
Finding peace in love's echo.

Tryst with the Rising Sun

In whispers soft, the morning breaks,
A dance of light, where silence wakes.
The horizon blushes, hues so bold,
A promise new, a tale retold.

Birds flutter high in vibrant flight,
Chasing dreams in the golden light.
With each heartbeat, the world exhales,
As dew-kissed grass tells hidden tales.

The sky ignites in fiery grace,
Awakening glow on every face.
With every ray, shadows retreat,
In the embrace of the sun's warm seat.

Moments flicker like candle flames,
In this stillness, we play our games.
The sun ascends, takes its throne,
In this kiss, we're never alone.

As day unfolds, we stand anew,
Beneath the sun's radiant view.
A tryst we share, you and I,
In the canvas of the waking sky.

Fanfare of the Dawn

The trumpet sounds as night departs,
Welcoming light with open hearts.
A symphony of colors blend,
As night's silence begins to end.

Clouds are painted in strokes of gold,
Each dawn a story yet untold.
The stars retreat, their duty done,
As we rise up to greet the sun.

Nature's choir begins its song,
To the rhythm where we all belong.
Morning's breath, both fresh and sweet,
A melody where worlds compete.

With gentle sighs, the earth awakes,
A tapestry that twilight makes.
The sun ascends, a radiant flare,
A fanfare bold, beyond compare.

In this embrace of light and air,
Hope ignites, dispelling despair.
Together, we face the day anew,
In the fanfare that beckons you.

Chasing Shadows into Light

In the twilight hours, shadows play,
Dancing quietly, fading away.
Beneath the stars, whispers ignite,
We chase the dreams into the light.

Through the whispers of the trees,
The soft caress of a gentle breeze.
Each shadow holds a secret near,
A memory woven, crystal clear.

As dawn approaches, darkness bends,
The night's melody softly ends.
With every step, the shadows flee,
Into the warmth, we long to be.

Hearts awaken, dreams take flight,
In the embrace of morning light.
Together we rise, hand in hand,
Chasing shadows across the land.

In the glow of the sun's ascent,
We find our peace, our souls content.
Chasing shadows, we unite,
In the dance of day and night.

Euphony of the Early Hours

In the hush of dawn, a song does rise,
Nature's chorus beneath the skies.
Gentle waves of sound, soft and light,
A euphony born of the night.

The brook murmurs, the leaves all sway,
In rhythm with the breaking day.
Every note, a promise so dear,
Echoes of hope, crystal clear.

Clouds drift softly, a canvas wide,
Painting dreams as the world feels tied.
Each bird's call a note in the air,
A symphony that we all share.

Light unfurls like a silken thread,
Weaving stories where hearts are led.
In the early hours, magic we find,
A song of life, gentle and kind.

As the sun climbs high into the blue,
Its warmth wraps us, a sweet debut.
In the euphony that nature brings,
We rise together, our spirits sing.

Melodies of the Rising Sun

The dawn whispers softly, a gentle hum,
Birds greet the morning, their songs come.
Colors awaken, a canvas so bright,
Wrapped in the warmth of golden light.

The world stretches wide, in hues of gold,
Stories of dawn in silence unfold.
With each fleeting moment, dreams take flight,
Embraced by the glow, hearts feel delight.

The sun rises high, casting shadows away,
New hopes are born with the break of day.
Nature sings sweetly in harmony's tune,
A dance of the sun under a silver moon.

As whispers of morning begin to fade,
The melodies linger in forest and glade.
Time dances onward, a waltz so pure,
Each note a promise, forever to endure.

With each turning moment, life finds its way,
The sun's warm embrace, a radiant ray.
Melodies echo in every heart's song,
In the arms of the morning, where we belong.

Horizon's Embrace

At the edge of twilight, the sky ignites,
A dance of colors in soft delights.
The horizon whispers secrets untold,
In hues of crimson and shimmering gold.

Day surrenders, a gentle retreat,
Stars begin twinkling, a shimmering sheet.
Clouds painted vividly in evening's glow,
Wonders unfold where wild dreams flow.

With each passing moment, shadows extend,
The night softly beckons, a whispering friend.
In the embrace of dusk, we find our peace,
A quiet surrender, a sweet release.

The world pauses, held in the night's care,
Magic unfolds in the cool evening air.
In every heartbeat, the rhythm prevails,
As the horizon's embrace tells timeless tales.

Underneath the vastness, the heart beats loud,
In the soft dark blanket, we feel so proud.
With dreams like the stars, endless and bright,
We dance with the shadows, wrapped in the night.

Daybreak's Enchantment

The sun tiptoes softly over the trees,
A gentle awakening, a teasing breeze.
Pinks and purples in the canvas above,
Each brushstroke whispers of hope and love.

Morning unfolds with a delicate sigh,
As dreams dissolve in the cobalt sky.
With every heartbeat, life stirs awake,
In the arms of the dawn, we learn to take.

The melody dances, a sweet serenade,
Sunlight cascades through a forest glade.
Birds flit and flutter, a joyful display,
Echoing laughter in morning's ballet.

Every petal glistens with dew's tender kiss,
In the magic of dawn, there's pure bliss.
Life's gentle rhythm beckons us near,
As we welcome the sunlight, free of fear.

Daybreak enchants with its limitless grace,
Inviting us onward, a timeless embrace.
With hearts wide open, we greet the new day,
In the dance of the morn, we find our way.

Softly Shattered Night

In the quilt of darkness, dreams softly weave,
Whispers of secrets that twilight believe.
Stars hang like jewels in the vast, deep sea,
With each twinkling story, they beckon to me.

The moon casts a glow through the windowpane,
A silvery shimmer in the quiet lane.
Gentle reflections of thoughts that appear,
In the soft shattered night, all becomes clear.

With each fleeting moment, shadows are born,
As silence embraces the coming dawn.
Mysteries linger, with soft, tender fright,
In the embrace of the softly shattered night.

Dreamers awaken, wrapped in their fears,
In the cradle of night, they shed silent tears.
Yet hope dances lightly, a flickering spark,
Guiding us gently through moments so dark.

When the stars whisper tales of times gone by,
And the world is painted with a soft sigh,
In the stillness of dark, magic takes flight,
In the heart of the soft, softly shattered night.

Illuminated Pathways

In twilight's glow, shadows play,
Each step forward, a night's ballet.
Stars whisper secrets, soft and clear,
Guiding lost souls, drawing near.

Moonlit beams on cobblestone,
Reflecting dreams, where hope is sown.
Footprints linger, stories untold,
In every corner, hearts unfold.

Through ancient woods, where silence breathes,
Nature's pulse in whispered leaves.
A path adorned with misted light,
Leading onward, into the night.

Beneath the arch of deepening skies,
The promise of dawn softly lies.
Every step, a chance to find,
Treasures hidden, love entwined.

With each turn, new visions bloom,
Illuminated, dispelling gloom.
And as we walk this endless way,
Hope illuminates, come what may.

The Bursting Sky

Crimson clouds begin to rise,
Painting dreams across the skies.
Beneath the canvas, hearts ignite,
As day transforms, embracing night.

Stars erupt, a dazzling show,
The universe begins to glow.
Galaxies swirl, a cosmic dance,
In the darkness, we take a chance.

Winds of change whisper through the air,
Stories linger, floating there.
In the chaos, beauty sings,
As nature weaves its vibrant strings.

The horizon bleeds with colors bright,
Each hue a spark in dying light.
A symphony of hues collide,
In this moment, we abide.

As the heavens burst and sway,
We find our place, we choose our way.
In the silence, listen close,
To the heartbeat of the cosmos.

Sunlit Sagas

Golden rays touch the earth,
Awakening life, a time of birth.
Every petal glistens, pure and bright,
Telling stories in the morning light.

Meadows dance in gentle breeze,
Nature laughs, inviting ease.
Every whisper, a humble song,
In this realm, we all belong.

Brooks babble with forgotten tales,
Carrying dreams on flowing trails.
Sun-kissed laughter fills the air,
Embracing warmth, joy to share.

Beneath the boughs of ancient trees,
Life's chapters flutter in the leaves.
Each moment drips with radiant glow,
A tapestry where we all grow.

As day unfolds, we find our part,
In sunlit sagas, heart to heart.
In every breeze, in every ray,
We write our story, come what may.

Greeting the Dawn

With breath held tight, the horizon wakes,
A symphony of light, the world shakes.
Brushstrokes of amber and gold,
Whispering secrets, softly told.

Morning dew clings to the grass,
As shadows retreat, they gently pass.
Hope unfurls like a new bloom,
Chasing away the remnants of gloom.

Birds rise high, a melodious call,
Echoing through the great expanse, tall.
In the stillness, dreams take flight,
In the embrace of the dawning light.

The world awakens, fresh and clear,
Each heartbeat spells the dawn near.
Golden rays, a promise made,
Inviting the light to cascade.

As we stand on the edge of day,
Embracing warmth in a vibrant way.
Greeting the dawn, we come alive,
In every moment, we thrive.

Lullabies of the Dawn

Soft whispers brush the trees,
Gentle sighs of the breeze.
Stars begin to fade away,
In the light of the new day.

Dreams dissolve in morning light,
Taking flight, a lovely sight.
Colors bloom in the soft sky,
As the night bids goodbye.

Birds awaken, sing their tune,
Greeting sun and silver moon.
Nature dances, calm and free,
In this moment, harmony.

Clouds drift slowly, painting grace,
In this tranquil, sacred space.
Hearts are lifted, hopes arise,
In the glow of brightening skies.

Lullabies of dawn embrace,
Every soul, a warm embrace.
Feel the peace, let worries cease,
In this new day, find your peace.

Joyful Rays of Morning

Sunlight spills on waking fields,
Golden warmth, the heart it yields.
Birds take flight, a joyful dance,
In the light, there's a chance.

Morning dewdrops gleam and shine,
Nature's jewels, so divine.
Colors splash in vibrant play,
Chasing shadows far away.

Every flower, fresh and bright,
Unfurling petals to the light.
Joyful whispers fill the air,
Promises of dreams laid bare.

Laughter echoes through the trees,
Carried softly by the breeze.
Hearts awaken, spirits rise,
With the sun that fills the skies.

Joyful rays of morning's glow,
Guide us where our hearts would go.
In this moment, let us stay,
Embracing love of today's play.

Harmony in the Heavens

Clouds drift gently, soft and white,
Kissing blue, merging in light.
Stars still glimmer in retreat,
As dawn rises, calm and sweet.

Whispers float on zephyr's breath,
Songs of life, a dance with death.
Every note a tale untold,
In the warmth, our hearts unfold.

Sunbeams glisten, painting skies,
Reflections of our hopes and sighs.
Harmony sings in the air,
Uniting all in love and care.

Mountains stand proud, high and free,
Guardians of the earth's decree.
In this realm, we find our place,
In the vast embrace of grace.

Harmony in the heavens bright,
Each heartbeat a spark of light.
Together, we rise and soar,
In the infinite, evermore.

Embrace of the Day

Morning glows with tender light,
Welcoming the day so bright.
Gentle breezes kiss the skin,
Whispers of the life within.

Trees sway softly, roots in earth,
Claiming joy, embracing worth.
Nature sings, a vibrant heart,
Holding close, we are a part.

Moments cherished, pure and sweet,
Every heartbeat, life complete.
In this dance, we find our way,
Underneath the skies of gray.

Hands stretched wide towards the sun,
In this place, we are all one.
Love surrounds in warm display,
In the embrace of the day.

Embrace of the day, let's soar,
Every moment, ask for more.
Fill your spirit, let it shine,
In this journey, yours and mine.

Dawn's Whispering Light

In the hush of morning's grace,
Tender beams begin to trace.
Nature yawns, the world awakes,
Whispers soft as daylight breaks.

Colors dance in golden streaks,
Birds call out, their joy unique.
Every leaf and petal glows,
In this light, serenity flows.

Winds that carry night's sweet song,
Now are gentle, soft, and strong.
As the sun ascends above,
All is wrapped in warmth and love.

Clouds are painted shades of gold,
Silent stories now unfold.
Dewdrops sparkle, fresh and new,
Every path invites a view.

Hope is woven in the dawn,
With the night, our fears are gone.
Embrace the day, let spirits rise,
In my heart, the promise lies.

Morning's Gentle Embrace

Softly flows the morning air,
Lifting dreams without a care.
Sunbeams kiss the sleeping land,
With a touch, both warm and grand.

Birds are singing, notes so bright,
Chasing shadows from the night.
Flowers bloom in radiant hues,
Glistening with the morning dew.

Paths of gold stretch far and wide,
Nature's beauty, a joyful guide.
Horizons beckon, wide and free,
Inviting all to simply be.

In the stillness, peace unfolds,
Whispers of the day retold.
Hope unfurls like petals near,
In this moment, love is clear.

Gather strength as daylight breaks,
In each breath, a chance remakes.
Hold the dawn close to your heart,
New beginnings, a fresh start.

Awakening the Golden Sky

With each dawn, the world ignites,
Colors blend in vibrant sights.
Warmful glow caresses all,
Nature answers every call.

Echoes of the night retreat,
As the sun, the day does greet.
Golden rays, a sweet embrace,
Washing over time and space.

Over hills where shadows lay,
Life begins to seize the day.
Each horizon glows anew,
Bringing promise, bright and true.

In this light, the heart expands,
Holding dreams within our hands.
Birds take flight, they soar and glide,
Painting skies where hopes reside.

The golden hour, all is bright,
Moments captured, pure delight.
As we dance with morning's grace,
Every heartbeat finds its place.

The Celestial Chorus

Stars begin their soft retreat,
As dawn unfolds, an ode so sweet.
Morning wakes with gentle sound,
In her arms, love knows no bound.

Clouds take flight in brilliant hues,
As the sky dons shades of blues.
Winds whisper tales from afar,
Nature's symphony, a guiding star.

Each ray paints a story bright,
Fill the silence with delight.
A chorus born from earth and sky,
Lift your spirits, let them fly.

Voices blend in harmony,
Every note, a memory.
In the beauty of this morn,
New hopes rise, from sleep reborn.

Gather close, the magic's here,
In the dawn, we shed our fear.
Join the song, let your heart sing,
In the warmth, new beginnings ring.

Dawn's Gentle Whisper

The sky blushes soft and warm,
As night retreats without alarm.
Birds chirp songs of sweet delight,
In the embrace of dawning light.

Hints of gold begin to spread,
Awakening all from their bed.
The world stirs with a tranquil grace,
As dreams dissolve without a trace.

Mist drifts low, a silent shroud,
Nature whispers, soft and proud.
Each leaf glistens, kissed by dew,
A canvas fresh, in vibrant hue.

Sunbeams dance upon the trees,
A gentle balm, a soothing breeze.
The day unfolds, a tale untold,
In warm embrace, we find our hold.

With every breath, the colors bloom,
Banishing shadows, clearing gloom.
Dawn's gentle whisper calls us near,
Inviting joy, erasing fear.

Awakening Light

As dawn appears, the dark recedes,
The world awakes from slumber's needs.
With tender grace, it takes its flight,
Awakening in the morning light.

Colors blush with each new ray,
Chasing the night's shadows away.
The brook sings softly, a lively tune,
As flowers bloom beneath the moon.

In every blade and petal fair,
The promise of the day is there.
Nature yawns and stretches wide,
As warmth and joy begin to glide.

Birds take wing on breezy paths,
In grateful songs, they share their laughs.
Awakening whispers fill the air,
With every heartbeat, a moment to share.

Hope rises high, like sunlit skies,
Chasing shadows, letting light rise.
Awakening light, a constant song,
Guides us gently all day long.

The Colors of Morning

Soft hues paint the waking sky,
As darkness bids its sweet goodbye.
A palette rich with vibrant dreams,
In the morning's golden beams.

Lavender mist and coral pink,
With every shade, the heart will sink.
Into the beauty, deep and true,
Of all the wonders that morning drew.

Nature stirs with gentle sighs,
As daybreak brings a sweet surprise.
Through every leaf and every flower,
Colors speak of spring's own power.

Birds of bright and vivid song,
Fill the air where they belong.
Each note a splash, a joyful sound,
In the embrace of beauty found.

The colors weave a tale so bright,
Of hope reborn in morning light.
In every hue and every shade,
The story of the day is laid.

First Light's Caress

First light breaks with gentle grace,
A tender kiss on nature's face.
It beckons all to rise and shine,
To greet the day, fresh and divine.

With a whisper, shadows fade,
As sunbeams dance in a warm cascade.
The horizon glows, a promise made,
Of new beginnings, unafraid.

Each flower opens, dressed in dew,
The morning's breath, a sweet debut.
In every corner, life returns,
With every heartbeat, passion burns.

Softly now, the world awakes,
With laughter pure, as morning breaks.
Each moment glimmers, shines anew,
In the soft embrace of the brightened view.

First light's caress, a soft refrain,
Guiding hearts through joy and pain.
With every dawn, new dreams arise,
In the magic of the morning skies.

The Awakening Chorus

In whispers soft, the morning calls,
As light breaks through the shadowed halls.
The birds begin their sweet refrain,
A world reborn from night's dark chain.

With every note, a spark ignites,
The colors bloom, the heart takes flight.
Each petal opens, fresh and new,
In nature's arms, we find our view.

The sun ascends, a golden sphere,
Dispelling doubts and all our fear.
The breath of life, it fills the air,
An echo of a love laid bare.

United voices, strong and clear,
Compose a hymn for all to hear.
In perfect harmony, we stand,
Together bound, hand in hand.

Each moment sings of hope's embrace,
In joy and peace, we find our place.
Awakening, we rise anew,
A chorus bright, forever true.

Light's First Dance

Upon the hills, the shadows fade,
As dawn unveils its radiant blade.
The dew-kissed grass begins to glow,
In gentle waves, the breezes flow.

The sun peeks out, a timid sight,
And warms the earth, dispelling night.
With every beam, the world ignites,
As nature sways to morning's rites.

In golden rays, the flowers sway,
Their petals lift, they greet the day.
A tapestry of colors bright,
In silence dances pure delight.

The sky awakens, painted blues,
With clouds that drift like whispered cues.
As light unfolds, the heart finds peace,
In this embrace, all worries cease.

Each moment flows, a sacred chance,
To join in nature's sweet romance.
As light's first dance takes center stage,
We turn the page, we feel the age.

Chorus of the New Dawn

A symphony of early light,
Welcomes the day, dispels the night.
In harmony, the creatures wake,
Awash in rhythms nature makes.

The rivers sing with joyful sound,
As blossoms flourish all around.
Each note a pledge, each sound a rhyme,
In chorus sweet, they mark the time.

The hills resound with voices clear,
Each echo pure, a song sincere.
In every heart, the music swells,
A tale of hope that softly dwells.

From silver streams to rustling leaves,
The world rejoices, the spirit cleaves.
Together in this sacred space,
We rise to meet the dawn's embrace.

With every breath, we weave our fate,
In nature's song, we celebrate.
The chorus of the new dawn sings,
A promise bright of wondrous things.

Celestial Blossoms

Beneath the sky, so vast and deep,
The stars above begin to creep.
Each glimmer shines, a unique spark,
In midnight's calm, they leave their mark.

The blossoms bloom in silken grace,
Reflecting light in a darkened space.
Their petals soft, like whispered dreams,
Unfolding hope, or so it seems.

The galaxies spin with gentle sighs,
As night reveals its lullabies.
In cosmic dance, the planets play,
Their timeless waltz, a grand ballet.

With every twinkle, tales are told,
Of journeys new and hearts so bold.
Celestial blooms of light and grace,
Embody love in vast embrace.

Together bound by starlit streams,
We chase the echoes of our dreams.
In floral hues and twinkling lights,
Celestial blossoms grace our nights.

Embers of the New Day

The dawn breaks soft and bright,
With hues of gold and red.
Whispers of the night take flight,
As shadows gently tread.

A promise lies in every glow,
The world begins anew.
With every sunrise, hope will grow,
Embracing morning's view.

The birds begin their cheerful song,
A melody of cheer.
As nature wakes, it feels so strong,
Dispelling all the fear.

The dew-kissed grass reflects the light,
While flowers start to bloom.
In this calm and wondrous sight,
The heart begins to swoon.

So let us greet this brand new day,
With open arms and glee.
For in the warmth of dawn's first ray,
We find our spirit free.

Dappled Light Play

In the forest, light does dance,
Through leaves that softly sway.
Nature sings a sweet romance,
In shimmering array.

Sunbeams peek through branches wide,
Creating magic bright.
Each shadow holds a secret guide,
A world of pure delight.

The brook reflects the twinkling sun,
As ripples play along.
Each moment here is just begun,
In nature's timeless song.

Wildflowers bloom with colors rare,
As wildlife frolics near.
The beauty found beyond compare,
Gives peace within our sphere.

So wander where the soft light falls,
And let your spirit soar.
For in this place where nature calls,
You'll find forever more.

Awakening the World

The dawn unveils a canvas wide,
As colors meld and blend.
The sleeping Earth, with arms spread wide,
Awakens with the friend.

Each creature stirs from dreams so deep,
Emerging with delight.
The rhythms of the world, we keep,
As day replaces night.

The air is fresh with minted dew,
Each breath a brand new start.
With nature's brush, the day we'll hue,
In every beating heart.

The mountains greet the sun above,
While rivers flow with grace.
In every glance, a sign of love,
As life begins to race.

So take a moment, breathe it in,
This life so vivid, true.
For in each phase, we all begin,
Awakening anew.

Sing to the Morning

Awake, my heart, to morning's call,
Let joy fill up the day.
With every note, let spirits rise,
And chase the night away.

The sun unrolls its golden thread,
Across the waking earth.
With every ray, new dreams are fed,
A canvas of rebirth.

The flowers sway, a soft ballet,
In harmony they bloom.
With every song the dawn will play,
Dispersing every gloom.

So join the chorus, feel the light,
Embrace what lies ahead.
For in this moment, pure delight,
Leaves no room for dread.

Sing out to morning, greet the day,
With voices clear and true.
For in this song, we find a way,
To dream and start anew.

Flickers of a New Dawn

In the east, the light begins,
A soft whisper, a gentle spin.
Colors dance on the horizon,
Flickers of hope in the dawn's embrace.

Birds take flight, their songs arise,
Melodies weave through painted skies.
Each ray a promise, fresh and bright,
Awakening dreams from the night.

Shadows linger, yet fade away,
As the sun heralds a brand new day.
Fields of gold greet every soul,
Filling hearts with warmth, making whole.

Morning dew on petals gleams,
Life awakens, stirring dreams.
Nature breathes, in harmony,
As life unfolds its symphony.

Hope unfurls in the daylight's glow,
With every heartbeat, blessings grow.
Flickers of joy, laughter and cheer,
A new dawn whispers, "I am here."

Morning's Gentle Touch

Sunrise kisses the sleepy ground,
With each breath, life's joys abound.
A golden glow warms the chill,
Morning's embrace, a soothing thrill.

Whispers of wind, so soft and sweet,
Nature's rhythms make us complete.
Birds chirp their joyous refrain,
In this moment, peace we gain.

Leaves fluttering, a gentle sway,
Inviting us to start the day.
Hearts awaken, ready to play,
In the light of morning's ballet.

Clouds drift lazily in the blue,
Each moment feels fresh and new.
Time slows, granting us a chance,
To savor life's exquisite dance.

Morning's gentle touch, a caress,
Fills our spirits with tenderness.
With every sigh, let worries part,
Embrace the dawn and open your heart.

Lullabies of the Daybreak

The horizon blushes, morning sings,
A tender hush as the new day brings.
Dreams dissolve in the golden light,
Lullabies of peace take gentle flight.

Softly rising, a world reborn,
Every shadow touched by dawn.
Hope is woven in every hue,
Mornings beckon with promises true.

Nature's chorus begins its play,
Awakening hearts with each soft ray.
Leaves whisper secrets of the night,
In daybreak's charm, we find our light.

As the sun climbs, shadows retreat,
Life unfurls in its rhythmic beat.
Hands reach out to grasp the day,
Lullabies guide us on our way.

A canvas painted with every hue,
Breath of new beginnings, pure and true.
In this moment, let go of care,
Lullabies of daybreak fill the air.

Early Morning Muse

In the quiet, a spark ignites,
Whispers of dreams in the soft light.
Pages open, the pen awaits,
Early morning muse, don't hesitate.

Thoughts awaken, fresh and clear,
Inspiration flows as skies appear.
The world is still, yet full of grace,
Hidden wonders find their place.

Sunbeams dance on the writer's page,
Crafting stories, setting the stage.
Words take flight, a soaring quest,
In the gentle dawn, creativity rests.

With each stroke, the heart knows peace,
Ideas blossom, worries cease.
Morning's canvas is wide and bright,
Early dreams take their joyful flight.

Embrace this magic, let it flow,
In the stillness, let your spirit grow.
Life unfolds in silken hues,
Early morning muse, share your views.

Daybreak's Kaleidoscope

Colors bloom in morning light,
Whispers dance through the night,
Shadows fade, the sun awakes,
Painting skies with gentle strokes.

Birds take flight on joyful wings,
Nature breathes, the new day sings,
Every hue a fresh embrace,
In the dawn's warm, tender grace.

Golden rays through branches soar,
Softly knocking on my door,
Each moment a vibrant thread,
In life's tapestry, we're led.

Clouds of grey drift far away,
Promising a bright new day,
In the sky, a canvas wide,
With every color, hope abides.

As the world begins to stir,
Silent dreams begin to blur,
In this kaleidoscope of light,
Hearts awaken, spirits bright.

First Rays of Hope

At dawn, the world takes a breath,
In the stillness, fears are left,
First rays kiss the waking land,
A gentle touch, a guiding hand.

Golden beams break through the gray,
Chasing all the night away,
With each flicker, joy ignites,
Gifting hearts with pure delights.

The sky blushes with promise new,
Every rise brings shades of blue,
Hope, like flowers, starts to bloom,
Filling every empty room.

Through the trees, the light cascades,
Life awakens, gentle glades,
In the warmth, dreams take their flight,
Born anew in morning light.

First whispers of a brand new day,
Rising softly, come what may,
With each moment, courage grows,
In the heart where love bestows.

Symphony of the Morning

Morning breaks, a soft refrain,
Birds compose their sweet campaign,
Leaves rustle in a gentle breeze,
Nature's song brings hearts to ease.

The sun peeks through the willow's grace,
Colors blend, a warm embrace,
Every note a vibrant seed,
Sowing love in every deed.

Pattering drops of morning rain,
A soothing sound, a sweetened gain,
Rhythms pulse with life anew,
In this symphony, I'll woo.

Clouds dance soft in skies of blue,
Painting dreams in every hue,
In this orchestra of light,
Hope plays on, a pure delight.

With each dawn, the world awakes,
Life's melody, the heart it stakes,
In this song, we find our way,
A symphony to start the day.

A New Day's Promise

The horizon glows with fire,
Whispers stir, hearts inspire,
Each dawn brings a brand new start,
With gentle peace that warms the heart.

In the light of morning's grace,
Dreams awaken, find their place,
Every shadow made to flee,
In the light, we find the key.

Hopes arise like birds on wings,
Joyful tunes that daylight sings,
With each moment, futures gleam,
Every dawn, a waking dream.

Promises of love unfold,
Stories waiting to be told,
In every sunrise, we find peace,
A moment's stillness, fear's release.

As the day begins to rise,
Countless wonders greet our eyes,
In the promise of today,
We find strength to guide our way.

Celestial Harmonies

In the night sky, stars align,
Whispers of love, softly divine.
Galaxies twirl, a cosmic ballet,
Playing the tunes of night and day.

Celestial bodies, they sing and shine,
Guiding the lost with a light so fine.
Every heartbeat, a note in the song,
Together in peace, where we all belong.

Moonlight dances, casting a glow,
Painting the earth in shimmering flow.
A universe vast, yet so close to heart,
In perfect rhythms, we each play a part.

Nebulas bloom, in colors so bright,
Eclipses embrace, then fade into night.
With every glance, the wonders unfold,
Tales of the cosmos, timeless and bold.

Let melodies rise, in harmony's grace,
Joining the stars in a celestial embrace.
Together we'll soar, on this musical sea,
Bound by the love that sets spirits free.

The Light of Possibility

A dawn so gentle, softly it breaks,
Awakening dreams, as the heart wakes.
In every shadow, a flicker of hope,
Guiding each soul on this vast, wondrous slope.

The light of possibility, shining so bright,
Illuminating paths, banishing night.
In whispered moments, a chance to reclaim,
The spark of creation, igniting the flame.

Colors of promise, painting the sky,
Each hue a reminder, we can always fly.
With courage aflame, we climb every height,
Embracing our dreams, in the warmth of the light.

As petals unfurl, the future awaits,
Opportunities bloom, as time dictates.
In fields of adventure, we run wild and free,
The light of possibility, guiding you and me.

So follow the glimmer, let doubt disappear,
In the dance of the moment, our purpose is clear.
Together we'll flourish, like stars in the night,
United in hope, we'll harness the light.

Dawn's Blissful Dance

The horizon blushes, as night bids adieu,
Welcoming warmth, in shades of soft blue.
Whispers of morning, with laughter imbued,
Dawn's gentle dance, a blessing renewed.

Golden rays stretch, to kiss the earth's face,
Nature awakens, in a beautiful grace.
Birds take flight, their songs fill the air,
Chasing the shadows, dissolving despair.

With every heartbeat, the world starts to rise,
Magic unfolds, beneath painted skies.
Through fields of blossoms, the breeze starts to play,
As dawn's blissful dance ushers in a new day.

In the shimmer of light, hope starts anew,
Each step a promise, in a world made for two.
Where dreams take shape, and wishes reside,
In the arms of the morning, we'll boldly glide.

So let us rejoice, in this moment sublime,
For within each dawn, lies the rhythm of time.
Embrace the beauty, let your spirit trance,
In the waltz of the sunrise, our hearts take their chance.

Rays of Renewal

In the still of the morn, the sun starts to rise,
Casting soft light, brushing tears from our eyes.
Each beam a reminder, of all we can be,
In the warm glow of hope, we finally see.

Rays of renewal, unfurling their grace,
Washing away doubts, as shadows embrace.
Every heartbeat pulses with life, bold and true,
A symphony plays, in colors anew.

Dance in the sunlight, let worries take flight,
In the arms of the breeze, find your delight.
With every step forward, we rise and we soar,
United as one, we discover our core.

As flowers awaken, perfumed and bright,
Their whispers of joy dance in morning light.
Through valleys of dreams, together we roam,
In rays of renewal, we find our true home.

So cherish the moments, as day turns to dusk,
In the warmth of our hearts, let love be the trust.
Embrace each sunrise, with laughter and cheer,
For with every dawn, new beginnings are near.

www.ingramcontent.com/pod-product-compliance
Ingram Content Group UK Ltd.
Pitfield, Milton Keynes, MK11 3LW, UK
UKHW021302280125
4330UKWH00005B/93